STOCK

STOCK

JENNIFER BOWERING DELISLE

COACH HOUSE BOOKS, TORONTO

first edition

Published with the generous assistance of the Canada Council for the Arts and the Ontario Arts Council. Coach House Books also acknowledges the support of the Government of Canada through the Canada Book Fund and the Government of Ontario through the Ontario Book Publishing Tax Credit.

LIBRARY AND ARCHIVES CANADA CATALOGUING IN PUBLICATION

Title: Stock / Jennifer Bowering Delisle.
Names: Delisle, Jennifer Bowering, 1979- author.
Identifiers: Canadiana (print) 20250233436 | Canadiana (ebook) 20250234793 | ISBN 9781552455104 (softcover) | ISBN 9781770568730 (EPUB) | ISBN 9781770568723 (PDF)
Subjects: LCGFT: Poetry.
Classification: LCC PS8607.E4844 S76 2025 | DDC C811/.6—dc23

Stock is available as an ebook: ISBN 978 1 77056 873 0 (EPUB), ISBN 978 1 77056 872 3 (PDF)

For Malcolm and Coralie

TABLE OF CONTENTS

ANY WORD IN BLOCKS

She recognizes the teeth. She thought, at first, they were selling her toothpaste, but now she sees the smile is for a business college. The head floats between a route map and a poem about bees by a local writer, sponsored by the city. Morphed by motion, by downtown, the teeth are little cars buzzing down the Main Line.

She saw the same teeth, she is sure, on Instagram that morning, smiling about real estate. As if they were inviting her to live inside a mouth.

The teeth belong to a woman who is attractive enough to be forgettable and forgettable enough to be relatable. She is a type, like a font, or blood.

Clock with a suitcase and a tampon. Stethoscope on a banknote, two coconuts in a bright pink bra. Any word in blocks. Slow becomes flow and chance becomes change and if you build a little house the bottom says insurance. Beautiful woman head beneath a boulder. Elephant on a tightrope and an ocean full of doors. Cat looks in a mirror and sees a lion. Chess pawn on the gallows, egg as light bulb and light bulb as window. Jar of money sprouting and for every page of matches

a brain made of human hands. If you wrap spaghetti on a wiener you get a barbell. Toothbrushes make love beneath a tissue blanket and how can we not find delight here, in these efforts to make metaphor? They try and fail, like poets. The businessman whose head is thrust in haystacks is a hand, offered across a gap of memory to an uncle's old cliché. And before we make the leap from the mantis on a keyboard to *computer bug*, we find ourselves in wonder at the bright

green creature

preying on

the M

MOTHER DAUGHTER SMILING HUGGING. CHILD GIVES FLOWERS FOR MOTHER'S DAY

Tulips pink as raw chicken
as knee where
pavement met skin
I love you special
offer daffodils
yellow as wax gently
scooped from tulip-pink ear
kitchen overexposed as
the woman who parents
in public put down
the phone stray hair
cerebral desires press
your forehead to hers
limited time
only to make the shape
of a heart with your bodies
and flowers
use the code MOTHER

CORPORATE MEETING. ATTRACTIVE BUSINESS PEOPLE WORKING IN MODERN GLASS OFFICE

This is the industry of blue.
A light that means business,
navy ethic
cyan cartridge of
tartar-fighting light.
Windex outlook
on corporate landscape,
the engineered air reflecting
company values   reflecting
          office into boardroom
holes   onto bodies
          square of light   deletes torso
ghosts type   in floor
          work seeps   out
                                        into   sky

BEAUTIFUL PICTURE WOMAN LOOKING AT SUNRISE OR SUNSET IN FIELD OF FLOWERS. ENJOY MOMENT

BEAUTIFUL WOMAN:

When I entered the sunflower field
my arms raised of their own accord.
The thousand petalled faces of my audience looked up
so I gave them each a car and the good news.
My hat was straw so I threw it to the sun
where it must have burned
because I never did find it.

At work, she is looking for a picture that connotes jurisprudence for occupational therapists.

She needs to show a couple buying insurance.

She needs a picture of an office computer being hacked to convey the importance of business continuity management (BCM).

She sees the woman again, first as doctor in a white coat, then as patient. She is giving bad news and then receiving it. There are 124 pages of results.

She is looking for a pharmacist whose eyes convey a hint of grief while laughing on a date.

She is looking for a pregnant carpenter who feels conflicted about bringing a child into a broken world.

She is looking for an ornithologist painting her bedroom the colour of a starling egg.

[FOUND POEM]: CATEGORIES

miscellaneous animal lifestyle nature business

family architecture food interiors
emotional signs/symbols

vector transportation people textures

abstract medical careers vintage education

curated celebrity science

object fitness industrial religion parks fashion sports

background art

[SEARCH]: WRITER

We wear mustard sweaters and tortoiseshell and if
we're blocked it's by the block of ice
in which our pencil has been lodged. There's always coffee
and quill and behold, a man in bed baring
his shaved chest to a typewriter.

This one types with right and writes with pencil in the left
composing both her novel and her Substack.

And this one, sinewed with tweed
elbow-patch blazer.
He has an oak desk. He has a pipe.
He has a wife who cuts his meat while he fleshes bloody plots
and sops the brilliance with his beard.

But I can blow the words from my palm toward the screen
like confetti, or a kiss.

There's paper crumpled round the laptop like snowballs
and it's okay because there's not a notepad in sight
and snow is good for poems.

[SEARCH]: FALL

Orange gourds and trees and fallen
seniors. So many ways of leaving
but none that make me feel the way
the weather does, like we've felt the last
breath of summer's false joy.
She holds her chest, she can't get up,
the cold was always already here.

CHEMICALS AND LIGHT

HAPPY HOUSEWIFE WITH WASHING MACHINE IN LAUNDRY ROOM WITH BASKET SNIFFING SHIRT

let's call you Sarah. Who keeps her soap
in wicker, who kneels before the front loader
caressing labour. Swept up
sheets and hair, oh Sarah
you are fresh spring, lemon breeze. White as rain.
What do you smile at in your basket?

SARAH:

People don't think of smiling as a skill.
But there's a trick
to the crinkle of the eye, angle of the head.
Instead of *cheese,* say *honey* –
it softens the jaw.

You are teaching your daughter
how to sniff the towel,
the terry umbilical between you.

SARAH:

There is no secret.
Just to catch them
being good and
separate your delicates
from your darks.

Who was it who said,
when a child is born
the mother is also born?
When I birthed her I became two,
the machine,
the basket.

I see my dust on your floors
I see my crust on your shirts
undeterred by detergent
or my weary efforts.
I see my face
as a stranger would,
hard as day.

GOOD MORNING, HAPPY FAMILY MOTHER FATHER CHILDREN PLAYING IN BED

Crisp Ts match the sheets and teeth.
No one peed or dreamed and Sarah,
you are rested. When morning came
you welcomed it to your bed, lifted it up,
called it sunshine, inhaled its breath.

SARAH:

I dreamt the moon went out like a street light
while I drove the kids to swimming. It was not
a nightmare, though there wasn't light to see
the people on the road, distortions of the dark.
I lost my way to the pool. One could make
too much of this – I had my clothes and teeth –
and my child was there, or my child
in someone's body and when she woke me
in the morning I didn't know who I was.

I keep thinking the word is *resentment*.
Knee in my back, snot shimmer
on my pillow. But perhaps it's guilt, Sarah,
wanting to make those tidy French braids,
wanting to greet them in the air.

SARAH:

She hates it when I do her hair.
She wants to see the braids, I never
angle the mirror right.
But I have a talent for smiling. Instead of cheese
say bestow. Instead of cheese say strive.

[FOUND POEM]: CATEGORIES 2

Mother icons
Mother symbols
Mother patterns
Mood and feeling
Mother designs
Mother borders
Working mother
Busy mother
Tired mother
Sad mother
Mother board
Asian mother
Black mother
Mother cooking
Mother nature
Mother backgrounds
Mother silhouettes

[SEARCH]: CRAFT

Symmetrical flames
stuck to the toilet paper roll
by floating hands.
Colour is primary.

Rules: lid the glue,
show don't run with scissors,
don't mix metaphors or you'll get brown.

This is the kind of craft
that will fly us to the moon,
that golden muse, tossing her botanicals.

My child's version shows the bleeding
of the marker, skid of glue
revealing where her hands were.
Is it the work that makes her proud
or does she really see a cat mewing on the page?

And does my poem mew? Does it fly?
Do you like it?
I made it for you.
It's not a *bird,* it's hope.

Share what you know
of fuel and jettison
and I'll show you where my hands were

my way of seeing
the night sky,
my way of saying, Look!

Look what I made!

HAPPY MOTHER AND CHILD SON IN THE KITCHEN BAKING COOKIES HAVING FUN

In matching aprons you make weather
out of flour and laughter.
I want that breeze
of mess and patience.

SARAH:

I once bought a picture of the dead on eBay.
The Victorians, it said, used special portrait stands
to prop their loved ones' bodies
as if they were still alive.
Children with stiff dresses and painted eyelids,
heads forcepped into life on metal posts.
I liked the ghost story shiver, creepy ringlets
and short pants. I liked the audacity
of a photographer disavowing
a most fundamental truth.
What else could a picture do,
with nothing but cast iron, chemicals, and light?

Sometimes I am not tender enough
to stay here while I sit here.
Dead battery, Monopoly.
A wish to play means a dish unwashed
or the knives of my own shoulders.

SARAH:

When I found out it's a scam, a myth
– those sitters were alive –
I felt both cheated and relieved.
The iron clamps were used
to help them remain still
for a long exposure. A pose,
a smile, too hard to hold.
A music stand can't support a body.
A face in death is swollen, not just bored.

Sometimes I do not want to play.
And sometimes in the art pile
with the unicorn
the smiling shark
there is me made of sticks.

SARAH:

Sometimes mothers were even draped
with sheets, to hold small children
squirming in their petticoats.
Only the mothers are the ghosts

HAPPY FATHER'S DAY! FAMILY MOM AND DAUGHTER CONGRATULATE DAD AND GIVE A GIFT

The couch is cropped but you
are pert as button tufts.
Your nails match the ribbon
and your daughter's dress.
He wears a brown turtleneck sweater
and you all peer in the open box. Watch,
necktie, macaroni'd picture frame.

SARAH:

Beneath my blouse I wear
a pretty effort, it's important
not to let things go except
the disappointments.

Mug, drill,
oracle. Knits to match the drapes
and paper, perfect trappings
of Love Glow lip gloss.

SARAH:

Beneath his smile he wears
a sorrow.
Beneath his sweater he wears
the world, sticking to the fibres
like a wound.

It's June, it's Father's Day,
only summer lies ahead
the perfect mug   glossy glow
it's June he wears   a thick sweater
knit smile

SARAH:

Our daughter already asking
for the box
to fill with rocks and ribbon
and the eraser shaped
like a heart.
Sometimes nothing
is so lonely as joy.

GOOD MOTHER MORNING FAMILY HAPPY

Her braids match the wicker's weave
the pop-song chorus
the kismet of a fiction
the lorem ipsum.

SARAH:
The language steers us wrong –
we say 'corners' of the mouth
but we must think not of points
but apertures,
invitations. Lip, not apex.

Coldest winter day, my own daughter's hair
(so fine, braids thwarted by cowlicks)
is on end. Carpet charges strawberry socks
and each strand reaches like a voice.

So I can only forgive my own mother
for my pigtails askew in every school picture,
which now I see was not carelessness but giving in
to the separateness of my body from her own.

And I can only feel wonder
at the force of the electric –
hair, heart.

CARA, THE MODEL:

The first time I came across my own face
was in a tweet about pandemic parenting.
'Ten Activities to Keep Kids Busy,' or something.
There I was, holding a paintbrush like a moustache
grinning at the kid grinning back at me
as if she were my own.

MOM DAUGHTER AT THE TABLE IN THE MORNING

SARAH:

I am an artist too. Look,
the bowl of strawberries, contrast
of red on white, life unstill.
And when they eat them, spilling
milk across the table,
I see the meaning: everything
is fleeting and worth cherishing.
The years are short and so are the days,
time flies and catches the worm.

Sarah, maybe it's not guilt your pictures bring
but loss.
What will I have squandered
when there's no lint trap full of stickers,
when my daughter no longer
cuts her drawing out,
leaving paper outlines curling
off the table like a skull?

SARAH:

Sure, I still sometimes
bring it out at parties, the portrait stand
a curiosity
of photography's early craft.

What will I have squandered
when their bodies have grown from milk
to muscle, bony backs felt
in rare enfolding,
when imaginations are encumbered
by the math of being?

SARAH ON FACEBOOK:
Here it is, the source
of the morning's percussion.
Pocket treasure little scamp. I swear
there'll be no stones left in the creek.

What will I have squandered
when my son needs
no help to read *anxious* and *collide*
and my daughter knows the difference
between *deaf* and *death*? Ohgod
when teeth have filled the space
that holds reports of love
and magic and attempts
to say *mythical* in lispy sorting
of the world?

SARAH ON INSTAGRAM:
It takes more muscles to frown
than it does to smile though I do
love a good workout lol

CARA:

He paid a hundred bucks
for the afternoon of shots. No royalties, no need
to bring any knowledge of lullabies or discipline,
just my own sweater with sleeves long enough
to cover half my hands when I held a mug between them.

AI-GENERATED SARAH:

There's a trick to holding the smile.
Instead of cheese say whiz.
The secret ingredient
is Love brand organic vanilla.

CARA:

And when I saw it, my image, at first
I didn't know why I recognized it. My own face
distorted by the kissy lips to hold the paintbrush
and the gaze of love I feigned so well.

Sarah, I'm starting to understand
it's not your patience,
it's your stillness. You can live here
in these smiles,
you never need to sleep,
the flour never falls to the floor.

AI SARAH:

Eat your vegetables all the
free range pluck
happens for a reason
don't roll your eyes at me
you don't know where I've been.

You remind me
to have a child is to feel
nostalgia for a time not past,
to feel them pulling away even
when they will not let you go.

AI SARAH:

smile   strawberries and
cookies and   stones it's
easy to dance like
someone is always watching

CARA:

How long we held it,
that empty box,
pretending it was full.

HOW NOT TO BE THE BIRD

The woman is there again on the side of the drugstore, hugging an elderly lady and a small child. Or is she the child, years ago? Or maybe she is the elderly lady, returned from the future to warn us of something we can predict but not fathom. Looking at them, she can't remember what year it is. How long has she been there, on the drugstore wall?

[SEARCH]: WINTER

It does not snow in the city
but you can become a woodland creature
if your knits are chunky

and forget there's danger simply
standing in the air
that your skin
is holding your life
like apples in a paper bag.

[ERASURE POEM]: LICENCE AGREEMENT

The entity on whose behalf you are entering
this time will change. Notice the means,
the automated renewals.
You agree to be bound to use
to other persons' content.
One natural person inside
acting in moving packs.
Motion means composition.
Master a series of sounds, now known
and hereinafter
still.

WAITING FOR THE JOB INTERVIEW. LEGS OF APPLICANTS IN A ROW OF CHAIRS, HOLDING RESUMÉS

JOB ID#6987638271
Join our team!

You are a reflection ninja
a go-glass-getter guru
experienced in the cerulean synergy
of ultramarine. Minimum 5000 kelvin.

Key Performance Indicators:

- Utilize azure
- Extrude indigo
- Pivot on the periwinkle

If this sounds like blue
reply to
Assistant Managing Director of Inc.

BEAUTIFUL BUSINESSWOMAN LOOKS OVER THE SHOULDER OF EMPLOYEE, POINTING AT COMPUTER

BEAUTIFUL BUSINESSWOMAN:

His hair smells like Excel
so I ask him to click on every picture with a bus.
I leaned in just like this to put down the pitcher,
maybe that's why I dreamed I was serving
at Chili's again. Fry grease stink
of KPIs and hustle beneath my cool
breeze antiperspirant. Trim the fax and Gantt the Sprint.
Zoom the Lessons Learned. Prep for performance
reviews, all hands, deliverable sales funnel
asset turnover harvesting market share
pro forma I forgot about table 10
they've been waiting thirty minutes. Hold the shift
control+option put the lean in
business canvas merit the increase in output
fudge cake hold the serif
Jack Spratt at the bored table asks for ketchup and I
always bring it.

JOB INTERVIEW. SHAKING HANDS IN OFFICE

When they ask, 'Where do you see yourself in five years?'
the right answer is never 'Here.' Nor is the right answer
the sea, though it's what you've seen
with what yogis call the mind's eye.
Your hem must rest between ambition and the knee
– just a suggestion of drive –
make them think of you with another
life, maybe a window. Do not wax about the bees,
whether it's to keep, or paint, or save.
They want to be your nectary, pod coffee,
Friday beer, hive mind. Don't reflect
on how long five years can be,
that some marriages are shorter, or your mother's fatal illness,
that a child who did not exist five years ago
can play the piano. Do not tally the weeks—
do not think about the 10,000 hours,
the 32 bee lifetimes, the floods, the new viruses.
Your hands must rest between your lap and your hope
– just a suggestion of fortune –
make them think of you growing
out your hair and bringing muffins, the wrong answer
is never 'Here' and the right answer is never
the forest, though you've dappled in it.

ATTRACTIVE BLOND FEMALE LEADER PEERS THOUGHTFULLY OUT HIGH-RISE WINDOW AND REFLECTS ON HOW FAR SHE HAS COME

ATTRACTIVE BLOND FEMALE LEADER:

When I was a kid
I thought all the public trash cans
said 'Thank You Mercy.' Didn't know French
but somehow vaguely knew
what mercy meant.

Have mercy on our lawn and the birds who choke
on bottle caps. Mercy on the garbageman
awash in Slushee and its wasps.

Mercy was a kneel,
a head bowed, a humility. To litter
was power, like the junior high kids with their smokes,
dropping wrappers on the path they wore
across the field, mittless, toqueless.
A power like the roar
of crotch rockets passing the station wagon,
the *Playboy* posters in the neighbour's garage.
The appeal was in flaunting disregard.

That was how to be
a grown-up. How to be someone
worth being in the world.
How not to be the bird,
how not to be the garbageman.
Dogs eat things on the ground
and also other dogs.

LADY BOSS SMILES WITH ARMS FOLDED

LADY BOSS:

Never cross your arms,
my father always said,
it's a sign of aggression.
Demonstrate active listening
with open posture,
steady gaze,
and all those pretty teeth
I paid for.

But it's my turn
to collect the dues.
Don't mistake this blazer
for a bosom,
no one coddled me
or paved my way.
And when the ceiling
is below you
in all its tempered glass
someone can still
see up your skirt.

Cross your arms,
my mother said, it's a sign
of aggression. Show them
all those pretty teeth
you've paid for.

CARA:

Ball-buster,
the photographer said,
and made a fist.
Don't you like
being on top?

Cross your arms,
he said. You
are confident.
Don't you feel confident?

Think of what you had to do
to get here.

[FOUND POEM]: KEYWORDS

Furniture woman
glass suit
luxury worker interior looking.

Folded inside company wall,
concrete window.

Thinking room
thinking view.
Wooden sky meeting real.

ILLUMINATED ENVELOPES FLOAT ABOVE A WOMAN'S HANDS TYPING ON A KEYBOARD

SUBJECT: Welcome to the Team!

As the Assistant Director of Envelopment and
Human Resource Extraction
I'd like to thank you for executing
the privilege of becoming a member
of our Kickback Start-Up
our Think K-Cup
our Little Family™.
Please find yourself attached.

FEMALE CEO IN PENCIL SKIRT STANDS ON THE MOUNTAIN SUMMIT

FEMALE CEO:

All through junior high I had the highest
bangs. Crown of Aussie Mega hairspray and nerve.
In high school I directed the school play
and they called me bossy so I made them trees.
Even then I knew this was a world of scarcity –
of Discmen and favour, tongues
worth letting down your throat, chances.
In university I bought promises like
the boys bought essays. When they were broken
I bought suits at Le Chateau.
I knew what to do with the straps
of my boots. I knew the way to the top
was crevassed with crass jokes and requests
to head the social committee. Now look down
at all the little trees in the valley
itching in their leaves.

[SEARCH]: LIGHT

This page is full of ideas.
Abstract neon, spot on a stage,
string of patio Edisons. He is credited
with an invention he only perfected,
the thinner, cheaper filament.
They say he slept three hours a night.
Tail lights motion blurred
pomodoro pendant, kanban floor lantern.
How to make the most of your workday.
Top 10 Productivity Hacks. Edison is credited
with sleeping in his closet in his clothes. Bullet
journal, inbox zero
how many words did you write today
beneath the LED flush mount?
Abstract digital connections
and the window's pattern on the floor.
The bulb was named for its shape
but tulips and onions also begin in dark.

COLLEAGUES WEARING MASKS BUMPING ELBOWS AT WORK

June 2021

O elbow bump, souvenir of first pandemic days
when people tweeted that *King Lear* was writ
in quarantine of plague, and made sourdough
and worried over handshakes and replacing them.
Yet you remain on the landing page of Zoom –
stock pic of chicken arms in business casual.
I'm not sorry that this office knock of bone
did not come to pass, but miss its innocence.
These models were first to learn to smile with eyes.
And photographers who rushed to shoot what seemed
a normal we might live in, new, but braced
by touch, were neither profiteers nor prophets
but humans hopeful for togetherness
and quick reprieve, even as they feared their breath.

[SEARCH]: MASK

Nurse, office worker, in this together. Server, grocer, beshorted deliverer, yes we are open orifices under cotton. Couples kissing, multicolour friends crowding in false lashes. Surfer, Statue of Liberty, gargoyle on the Notre Dame, baby chick, chihuahua. Pumpkin, cat. Cake topper. Ben Franklin on the hundred. Index finger. Piggybank, piggytailed child. Skeleton, soccer ball, Lincoln on the five terrier beagle Apollo Santa snowman mouse egg bride Beautiful Woman curves and how to bend them blue medical-eyed disposable face thumbs up if you're too close garbage can we are open we are open.

CYBERSECURITY CONCEPT. GLOWING LOCK ICON ABOVE KEYBOARD

In what city did your parents meet?
On what street did you grow up?
If you could be any bird, which would you choose?
When did you first learn about death?

> Please enter a password with
> a capital city
> a special someone
> a combination of letters and postcards
> at least eight characters and settings

When was the last time you read out loud?
Would you rather be alone or in a crowd?
Would you rather see with your ears or hear with your eyes?

> Password must have
> a chorus
> a transom
> a fulcrum
> a weft
> a carotid artery
> a carburetor
> a deus ex machina

When was the last time you walked in a forest?
To what song do you know all the words?

NETWORKING. SMILING WOMEN IN SUITS AT RECEPTION

True work-life balance is a cocktail plate and wineglass while she shakes your hand, tells you about her kitchen renovation the EDI initiative and the back-ordered dishwasher and inflation and the perfect storm, her smile a dangling lanyard.

She's been around long enough to know it was only a matter of hummus and Chardonnay and ticking all the right boxes and restructuring the org chart. The writing's on the wall and don't forget, that's travertine anyway there's Jim she needs to say hello but it's a pleasure.

You don't say you've met before. Yours is a face she can't place – she'll hold it nimbly till she finds a sill to leave it on.

STRESSED EMPLOYEE HOLDS FOREHEAD WHILE BOSS STACKS FILES ON HER DESK

I'd like to see you leverage
the cheek muscles on the happiness vertical more,
operationalize the teeth
in an omni-channel output. Remember,
you are the face of this company
and our company is so pretty
when your lips engage all stakeholders.

BUSINESSWOMAN POINTING GUN IN KILLER BOSS ATTITUDE

FROM: Chief Officer of Strategic Compliance
SUBJECT: Corporate update

You know I always shoot from the hip and you have all been killing it here are the bullet points our guerrilla marketing campaign was on point in putting a stranglehold on our target demographic we have not only hit our annual targets we are at the bleeding edge of the revolution in disruptive tech and pioneers in stunning design we have boots on the ground in the west and armed with a new product offensive and tactical deployment our branding will penetrate the market annihilate the competition and dominate the global sphere you have your marching orders any questions shoot me an email fire a Slack remember to get expenses in Friday is the drop-dead—

[SEARCH]: PAIN

Pain is red and mostly
in the back.
Pain is read by touch,
hands framing vertebrae
lit like Christmas lights.
But sometimes pain

is in the neck or knee.
Put your hands there
where it is red, you are read
by wince, skin opening
to show
the joint in flame

that the one in pain
is always alone.

WOMAN'S HANDS CUP ENVELOPE ICONS

SUBJECT: Annual Forecast

As the Executive VP of Syntax
I am pleased to pronounce that we
will execute semiotic synesthesia
in the first quatrain. Beginning next week
we will deploy economy of scansion
and disrupt the prosody of the anaphoric
scrum. In light of recent metrics
we plan to facilitate the dactylic fricative
in an omniscient-channel Return On Invocation.
If you have any rhetorical
questions please don't hesitate.

RULE OF THUMB

The smile follows, slowly, from the side of a bus. It asks what she's doing for dinner. 'I'm going home,' she says.

'Why not try our new crispy chicken?' asks the bus. She doesn't reply. 'Bitch,' says the bus.

[SEARCH]: SPRING

Bouquets on barnwood and bokeh on buds.
Cherry blossom toothache.
Where is the brown grass matted with mould
and sand of winter's traction,
the mophead shrubs, runoff lit
by littered foil, not the yellow of little boots?
Where, the mud-stiff gardening gloves worn
for warmth, the neighbours reckoning
that tomorrow, tomorrow that last ice will be gone,
the huddle of ladybirds under last year's leaves
mumbling *are we there yet* in their sleep?

[SEARCH]: BEAUTIFUL WOMAN

Beautiful women always touch their faces
as if the hands belong to someone else.
As if they're always being touched.

As if gazes are fingered,
skin around nerve.
Beautiful women always touch their faces,

onanistic skin care halting aging
in a still, afternoon breath
as if they're always being touched

by dew and perfect light
and admiration.
Beautiful women always touch their faces

as if nosing into form,
adding clay or removing stone,
as if their being comes from touch

and perhaps it does. Touch of mother, of sun,
infant grabbing chin, blush and smog.
Beautiful women pull their wrinkles taut

as if life is not their sculptor
as if their beauty's not their life
always being touched

by joy and grief and tripping through the world.
Falling happens in both love and time
and beautiful women hold up jowls

because they want there to be more.
They caress the softening folds of cheek
as if they're always being touched

by all the tender lovers of their lives,
by the fitful loving of their own selves.
Beautiful women always touch their faces.

BEAUTIFUL WOMAN EATING SALAD

(or, Why I Laughed)

Because it told a joke about a snowman smelling carrots.
Because it did an impression of a Jello mould.
It performed a one-woman satire about toxic masculinity
called *Green Goddess Dressing.*
It dropped five F-bombs in a rant about airplane food
and stroked an organic cucumber.
It got locked out naked in the rain while my mother was visiting
and then it told me it had always loved me and I cried
while I laughed, dabbing at my mascara,
and it got kicked in the tomatoes.

[SEARCH]: PARTY

100 per cent chance of confetti (POC).
Monsoon season.
Colour precipitates to patent shoes
flows to Pulp's 'Common People'
vapes by the light of the disco sun
clouds judgment and acne
falls and falls.

ENTHUSIASTIC CHEERFUL BEAUTIFUL WOMAN GIVING THUMBS-UP

This is the rule of thumb
taught at the national park –
if you can't cover the bison
with thumb straight out,
you're too close.

They graze and taste
like beef and gore
like they know it.

But you're the one gazed at,
shot in busty bright tee.

I read once that phrase
was an old law on the width
of cane allowed
for beating wives.
Rule of thumb. But that's
just a story, made up
to tickle the horns.

It's this, they say,
and how we oppose them
that separates us
from animals.

CARA:
Thumbs up and smile,
the photographer said,
it's universal.

Yet not with elbows locked.
Not in countries where
it denotes thrusting,
assholes.

But I held my arms out
till they ached,
I held my smile
like I held my breath
in the police procedural
in which I once played
the naked dead.

Great, he said. Tell me
everything is great.

[SEARCH]: HEELS
(or, What Heels Can Do Without Bodies)

Wave hello.
Mop the floor. Hold up gifts   walls
shape the curve and stretch the seams
and shop online for more.
Rule steps   cobblestones
swim and go horseback riding.
Stop a soccer ball. Stop a disco ball cool
out car window then check under the hood.
Lean on traffic cone and
sledge   anything you can
bike and hike and kick
climb ladders   mountains   grind
neckties into floor or
inflatable chests   I can do in
shrink men to mouse size   cowering
at spike and kitten
strap   peer over
cliff   unmembered
debodied
deheaded

WOMEN'S SECRETS. CLOSE-UP SHOWING A SIGN OF SILENCE

Her eyes are cropped. She'll see no evil
nor let it escape her mouth.
But why Sharpie 'shhh' across her finger
already pressed to puckered lips?

CARA:

Wait, he said. Leaned in,
wrote it with my finger still
pressed to my face. His hot
breath reeked of old coffee
and permanent ink.

He's sure I won't object,
assumes 'model' comes
from clay.
We want them to know you
have a secret.

Even though I killed them, I
fucking love dandelions.
Sometimes, I melt chocolate
chips on toast. And when you
leaned in, I saw the hairs
curling from your nostrils and
thought, you are the hooves
in this sausage.

shhh or else we'll think
her finger is a gun.

YOUNG PARTY GIRL COCKTAIL GLASS ON WHITE BACKGROUND

Of all the women who've sat in a martini glass,
you're the only Olive.

Some of us fell there, surprised,
splashing. Our stilettos kick carefree,
we hold fruit.

Find us in every colour
of dress and skin, but you
are crouched, coiled. You are pit

pissing in their gin.
The gently pubic triangle of glass
will shatter under your shoes

CARA:
When he said go for it,
I thought jugular.

[FOUND POEM]: KEYWORDS 2

Cheerful biology
adult growth
men care horizontal.

Men plant people
gardening human hands.

Men seed global springtime
people planet-space

water responsibility
clean protective sportswear.

Vitality forest
dirt development –
only nature.

EXPLORE VISUALS CREATED WITH THE POWER OF AI

In a dim oak library
a robot holds a quill
and writes on parchment
already stained with lemon
and burned around the edge.
I'm told my creativity
can be unleashed.

AI has made its self-portrait
its Tinder profile,
celestial eyes, shirtless
baring rippling blue networks
while its real body
is a catacomb
of stacked silver boxes
flickering on a barren farm.

This form, its flexes,
more human than generated friends
with half heads
and hands where noses go,
more human than the girl
gently pinked
who does not live
but can be owned,
whose smoothness frames lips
slightly parted as if about
to be silenced.

GROUP OF FEMALES PROTESTERS MARCHING ON THE ROAD. WOMAN HOLDING A SIGN ABOUT WOMEN EMPOWERMENT

The sign she holds above her head
just says WOMAN.
Label for a museum diorama. Stuffed
denim, blond dreadlocks,
beauty unencumbered
by flannel or shouting. What's to protest
when you're on the pill? Capitalize
on controversy without being controversial.
The RED FOX lives in prairie and parkland,
where its omnivorous diet changes with the seasons.
The CANADA LYNX makes its home in the boreal forest
where it dens in dense brush. Capture
drugstore aisle of skin tones, green
screen the intersection. What's to protest
when you're beautiful and beheld?
Identified by distinct cheekbones
and bare shoulders in summer. Look
how he placed their bodies in the frame
to make it seem like there's a crowd.
The SNOWSHOE HARE still runs across the snow
as it did when I held hands with Bonnie F.
in corduroy and name tag stickers. Look
how they made it seem like it is leaping.

[SEARCH]: RIGHT

June 2022

Direction arrow isolated.
Woman shouting into bullhorn.
Man pointing to the right.
Green ✓ and red X white background.

Woman shouting into bullhorn.
Cropped fists in air.
Green ✓ and red X white background.
How long into the night would I have bled?

Cropped fists in hair.
Blind Justice statue in lipstick.
How long into the night will she bleed?
How much dead tissue outweighs my life?

Blind Justice holding bathroom signs.
How much would they have made me bear?
How much dead tissue outweighs our lives?
Who carries the heft of their hate?

How much will they make us bear?
Man pointing to the right.
Who carries the heft of their hate?
Direction arrow isolated.

[FOUND POEM]: SEARCH FILTERS

Start your free trial.
Enter
a comma-separated list.
Number of people.

Show solid backgrounds.
Most relevant people.
Most popular ethnicity.
Only authentic gender
safe orientation
maximum size.

Number of people to exclude
panoramic.

Mood.

THE SHAPES YOU KNOW FROM MAPS

She finds the woman in the mandatory annual online course on Information Security. She is Susan, who left her computer unattended when she went to lunch and caused a reportable security incident.

1. *What is 2-factor authentication?*

    A. *The coordination of the two hemispheres of the brain*
    B. *Smelling colour, also known as synesthesia*
    C. *The dual systems for locating pain and registering the sensation of pain*
    D. *All of the above*

2. *Match the following terms to their definition:*

Data centre	*Memory*
The beach	*Firewall*
Phishing	*Bleach bottle*
Save	*Styrofoam*
Garfield phone	*Lyric*

[SEARCH]: CARE

Did I stand like that
when you were dying,

gentle daughter
kindly senior
all teeth and good light

behind you
above you
so you had to twist
to see my face?

You could not twist.
But maybe we did, smile
like that.

We all know care
is something you take

like a champ
like a man.

[SEARCH]: GRIEF

Grief is in the fingers.
A little creature caught across two laps
or held up to the mouth
as if for kissing
or consuming.

When I was young you often stood
with hands in a sink of water
trying to warm them. Even then
your body was failing you
in its task of milling blood.

My child did not notice
he wore two left-hand mitts all afternoon
and I never knew how much of grief
was seeing what the dead are missing.
The lost one's loss.

Grief's image is in blisters
from the monkey bars
fingers wondering little stars
little creatures caught across two laps.

[SEARCH]: ENGINE

Black crustacean crouched beneath its hood
cylinder head, carapace
fuel injector mandible.
How they found a shape to make in light
for this

sign of an unknown signified –
loose wire, failing sensor, failing god
sign of an unknown future

combustion chamber coiled cheliped
red cap like a claw already cooked.

[SEARCH]: SUMMER

Still life of flip-flops, straw hat,
pineapple wearing sunglasses. Palm
on beach without season. Clams baked
in low tide by a dome of heat,
berries cooked on the bush, seniors
sleeping on tile floors waiting for the ambulance
that does not come. The earth showing seams
like an old shirt worn and bleached again
and again. Put the shades
on the coconut and look: this beach
will soon be submerged by precedents
and the fire makes a cloud
whose lightning starts more fires.

7,888,365,123 ROYALTY-FREE EARTH IMAGES

EARTH:

You've put me in
so many hats.

Hard, straw, top, cop, Santa, birthday,
mortarboard, ball cap, helmet,
gas mask. Okay
that last is a little on the nose
– or should I say
a little on the Horn of Africa.

Watch out for arms that spring
from California and Nepal –
your planes like flies and I
am waving.

If I am to be a body
make me as Canova sculpted Cupid,
beautiful, powerful
smooth as marble and slow jazz.
Not this emoji frump,
SpongeBob grin. But sure,
carve me a smile
if you fear my heat,
my flood. If you need
to look me in an eye
to see my life.

I'm always being cupped
in hands with no bodies.
Grinning cuticles and soft
knuckles. Sometimes
your arms wear a suit. Sometimes
your arms evoke god
glowing in the dark,
the omniscient city.

Sometimes they pass me to a child.
I'm offered up as gift, tied
with ribbon like a kitten
or an artifact.

If I am to be a body
why not a dragon?
Breath of fire, hurricane in a wing beat
equally imaginary.
You can try to tame me
with a beautiful queen or a Viking child
you can try to blame me
for the dead sheep,
the singed field.

Instead you drop me
in meadows, grassy nests,
the pages of an open book. On beaches
amidst styrofoam and plastic,
piles of ash. Sometimes
I float in my own sea
like a heart inside a vein
like a mouth upon a tooth.

I am Earthlet.
Cities thrust from my crust,
sky-penetrators.
Or I'm cleaved at my equator
with smokestacks swelling from my core.
And it's not far off –
the mass of things you've made
is now greater than the mass
of all the living things.

If I am to be a body
look down
find my flesh under your feet.
You can do it if you squint, see
how roads follow contours
of my muscle.
The concrete cracks like winter skin
and beneath, the pink of things you try
to reign. Roots
ready to release their volunteers
and all around the life light enough
to float on wind, bee bum.

From space, I am the stars.
Ursa Major in the cities
of the eastern seaboard.
And you can choose
whether to take comfort in this view of home
or to see danger here, hubris.

See the shapes you know from maps
that mark the surface
of your lives. The light you make

and fling into the dark.
Just who is it
you mean to save?

If I am to be a body
make me to last,
make me as ctenophore,
the jellyfish who's spent
700 million years waving
rows of cilia,
who makes its own light
and shines it through the prism
of its body. Yes, a rainbow
in the deepest ocean.

Half a billion years ago,
the first with more than one cell
striated rock like brush strokes.
In another billion
some other cells may paint me
in their own image.
And I'll remember you
like you remember
a lost T-shirt,
a day at a lake. Fleeting,
pleasant enough,
all the swimming
the sunburn
the watermelon full of sand.

She buys a picture frame at the dollar store because it already holds someone she is certain she knows.

AUTHOR'S NOTE

All of the images, search results, and metadata referenced in this book are real. Some images described are composites of several similar photographs, while others are representative of visual clichés that are endlessly reproduced by different photographers. Titles were rewritten to mimic the typical keyword-laden image tags in stock databases.

Stock image databases such as Shutterstock and iStock are the source of many of the images in print and digital publishing and advertising, from the generic business people on billboards, to the Earth Day illustrations adorning store newsletters, to the endlessly meme-ified young woman and her boyfriend with the wandering eyes. Typically, subscribers may download royalty-free images for an annual subscription fee. Photographers upload their images, attach descriptions with keywords, and are paid by the download. Models who appear in stock photos are paid a flat rate for the photography session and do not earn royalties. Stock sites have also introduced generative AI, with the ability to create images of people who do not exist at all. While at the time of writing this tech is still in its infancy, often generating images that are nonsensical and grotesque, it raises serious concerns about both artistic copyright and representation.

Stock's low-cost model means that stock imagery is ubiquitous in our lives. It is a reflection of what (or who) is valued, of biases and privileges. In turn, stock imagery shapes, if only subconsciously, how we as a society interact and even define ourselves and each other.

– Jennifer Bowering Delisle, 2024

ACKNOWLEDGEMENTS

This book was written in ᐊᒥᐢᑲᐧᒋᐚᐢᑲᐦᐃᑲᐣ Amiskwaciwâskahikan, in Treaty 6 and Métis Region 4, home and gathering place for diverse Indigenous peoples including nêhiyaw, Dene, Anishinaabe, Nakota Isga, Niitsitapi, and many others. I am honoured to create here, and attempt to do so with respect, humility, and gratitude. Indigenous peoples have been grossly underrepresented and misrepresented in stock imagery. We must expect and demand better from these databases.

Endless thanks to Lisa Martin, Rayanne Haines, and Jannie Edwards for the generous and thoughtful feedback, wisdom, and inspiration. Your friendship is a tremendous gift, and this book would not be what it is without you.

Thanks to Gary Barwin for the feedback and mentorship, and for helping me experiment and play on the page instead of spinning circles in my head. Thanks to Elee Kraljii Gardiner and the Vancouver Manuscript Intensive for providing the space to explore this work in community.

Thanks to Claire Kelly, Wendy McGrath, and Matthew Stepanic for your feedback on many of these pieces and for your friendship. I am also grateful to members of the League of Canadian Poets' Parenting Poets Community for conversation and support through setbacks and celebrations, rejections and wins.

Thanks to Susan Holbrook for championing this book and for editing it with a keen and enthusiastic eye. I am honoured that Coach House Books has given this project a home and am grateful to all the staff.

Versions of these poems have appeared in the following publications:
'[Search]: Grief' in *Long Con* (as 'Grief').

'Colleagues Wearing Masks Bumping Elbows at Work' in *Quarantine Review* (as 'Sonnet for the Elbow Bump').
Thank you to the editors.

Funding for this project was generously provided by the Alberta Foundation for the Arts and the Edmonton Arts Council.

Behind this and most pieces of art are many hours of both visible and hidden labour, including generating income, parenting, running a household, and self-promotion. I am extremely privileged to have a supportive family and a reliable income that provides stability, comfort, and space for me to write.

Thanks, finally, to Kenton, Malcolm, and Coralie for your encouragement, inspiration, and love.

Jennifer Bowering Delisle's collection of lyric essays, *Micrographia* (2023), won the Robert Kroetsch City of Edmonton Book Prize and the Writers Guild of Alberta Memoir Award. She is also the author of *Deriving*, a collection of poetry (2021), and *The Bosun Chair*, a lyric family memoir (2017). She is on the board of NeWest Press and lives in Edmonton on Treaty 6 territory.

Typeset in Arno Pro and Garage Gothic.

Printed at the Coach House on bpNichol Lane in Toronto, Ontario, on Zephyr Antique Laid paper, which was manufactured, acid-free, in Saint-Jérôme, Quebec, from second-growth forests. This book was printed with vegetable-based ink on a 1973 Heidelberg KORD offset litho press. Its pages were folded on a Baumfolder, gathered by hand, bound on a Sulby Auto-Minabinda, and trimmed on a Polar single-knife cutter.

Coach House is located in Toronto, which is on the traditional territory of many nations, including the Mississaugas of the Credit, the Anishnabeg, the Chippewa, the Haudenosaunee, and the Wendat peoples, and is now home to many diverse First Nations, Inuit, and Métis peoples. We acknowledge that Toronto is covered by Treaty 13 with the Mississaugas of the Credit. We are grateful to live and work on this land.

Edited by Susan Holbrook
Cover and interior design by Crystal Sikma, cover image Shutterstock
Author photo by Zachary Ayotte

Coach House Books
80 bpNichol Lane
Toronto ON M5S 3J4
Canada

mail@chbooks.com
www.chbooks.com